DISASTER SCIENCE

THE SCIENCE OF AN EARTHQUAKE

LOIS SEPAHBAN

Published in the United States of America by Cherry Lake Publishing
Ann Arbor, Michigan
www.cherrylakepublishing.com

Consultants: Jennifer Rivers Cole, Department of Earth and Planetary Sciences, Harvard University;
Marla Conn, ReadAbility, Inc.
Editorial direction: Red Line Editorial
Book design and illustration: Design Lab

Photo Credits: Sadik Gulec/Shutterstock Images, cover, 1; Anthon Jackson/Shutterstock Images, 5; Dorling Kindersley/
Thinkstock, 7, 10, 13; Richard Ward/Dorling Kindersley RF/Thinkstock, 11; Deanne Fitzmaurice/San Francisco
Chronicle/Corbis, 14; Design Lab, 17; iBird/Shutterstock Images, 18; AFLO/Nippon News/Corbis, 20; Roger Ressmeyer/
Corbis, 23; Pallava Bagla/Corbis, 24; Shakil Adil/AP Images, 27

Library of Congress Cataloging-in-Publication Data
Sepahban, Lois, author.
  The science of an earthquake / by Lois Sepahban.
    pages cm. -- (Disaster science)
  Audience: Age 11.
  Audience: Grades 4 to 6.
  Includes bibliographical references and index.
  ISBN 978-1-63137-629-0 (hardcover) -- ISBN 978-1-63137-674-0 (pbk.) -- ISBN 978-1-63137-719-8 (pdf ebook) --
ISBN 978-1-63137-764-8 (hosted ebook)
  1. Earthquakes--Juvenile literature. 2. Earthquakes--Safety measures--Juvenile literature. 3. Earthquake prediction--
Juvenile literature. I. Title.

QE521.3.S47 2015
551.22--dc23   2014004035

Cherry Lake Publishing would like to acknowledge the work of
The Partnership for 21st Century Skills. Please visit www.p21.org
for more information.

Printed in the United States of America
Corporate Graphics Inc.
July 2014

ABOUT THE AUTHOR

Lois Sepahban has taught every grade from kindergarten to high school. She grew up in California
and remembers waking during the night to the shaking of the Northridge earthquake of 1994. In
her free time, she reads books, writes stories, and rescues animals.

TABLE OF CONTENTS

CHAPTER 1

RUMBLING IN THE DESERT

Not many people live in the desert district of Awaran, Pakistan. Those who do live in mud brick houses. A lack of rain makes farming difficult. Towns are spread far apart. Few regular roads connect the towns. Still, people make a living in Awaran, herding sheep and growing wheat where they can.

On the morning of September 24, 2013, the people of Awaran went about their daily lives. There were no clues that this day would be different from the day before. There

Pakistan features beautiful landscapes, but its natural disasters can be deadly.

was no strange weather. There were no unusual smells or sounds in the air. Everything seemed to be normal.

About 13 miles (20 km) beneath the ground near Awaran, though, things were not normal. Stress was building up in Earth's crust. On September 24, it was ready to explode.

That afternoon, an earthquake began shaking the town. Buildings collapsed and roads broke apart. People ran from buildings if they could. Nearly 500 miles (800 km) away in

BELOW THE CRUST

Earth is made up of three major layers. The top layer is called the crust. The middle layer is called the mantle. Near where it meets the crust, the mantle is solid rock. The extremely hot innermost layer is called the core. As the mantle gets closer to the core, it becomes so hot the rock melts into liquid. The core is solid, though. Scientists believe it is made of the metals iron and nickel.

the country of Oman, items on tables and shelves shook. The earthquake lasted for just one minute.

When the minute was over, the world had changed for the people of Awaran. By the end of the day, 328 people were dead and more than 440 were injured. About 90 percent of homes were destroyed, forcing survivors to sleep outside. Water was filled with mud, making it unsafe to drink. Food was buried under collapsed buildings.

THE LAYERS OF EARTH

This diagram shows the layers of Earth. After reading about the layers, what did you imagine they looked like? How does seeing this diagram help you better understand how the crust relates to the rest of Earth's layers?

For many people who do not live in earthquake zones, earthquakes may just be scary news stories. But for the people they affect, earthquakes are terrifying real events. Earthquakes are powerful. They destroy towns and collapse buildings. They raise mountaintops and create land that didn't exist before.

Earthquake scientists rushed to Pakistan to study the Awaran earthquake. They hoped to learn more about how and why earthquakes happen, to be able to better predict when and where the next one would hit.

CHAPTER 2

WHAT IS AN EARTHQUAKE?

Unlike shaking caused by humans, such as explosions or drilling, earthquake shaking is caused by the movement of tectonic plates along **fault lines**. Tectonic plates are a set of many drifting surfaces that make up Earth's crust. Fault lines occur and mountains form at the borders between these plates. When plates move past each other at fault lines, earthquakes can happen.

An earthquake is often made up of several smaller quakes. Sometimes there are foreshocks, or smaller shakes that happen before the main earthquake. Scientists do not know at first whether a shake is a foreshock. They wait to see if a larger earthquake follows. They make observations and recordings. If a stronger earthquake follows, then scientists know that the first earthquake was a foreshock.

The biggest shake is called the mainshock. It causes most of the damage in large earthquakes. Mainshocks are almost always followed by smaller quakes called

MEASURING EARTHQUAKES

Seismometers are machines that record vibrations in the ground. Scientists use them to detect earthquakes and measure their power. Earthquake **magnitude** is compared using two scales. One, the Richter scale, works best for small earthquakes. The other, the moment magnitude scale, takes different measurements into account and works best for bigger earthquakes. Each step on these scales releases 32 times more energy than the previous step. So, a 7.0 earthquake releases 32 times more energy than one at 6.0. The Awaran earthquake measured 7.7 on the moment magnitude scale.

aftershocks. Scientists have observed that strong earthquakes have more aftershocks than mild earthquakes. Aftershocks often take place in the days after a mainshock. But they can also happen much later. Sometimes they take place months or years later.

Scientists take measurements to figure out whether a shake is an aftershock instead of a brand-new earthquake. First, scientists measure the **rupture** front of the earthquake. The rupture front is the exact location where

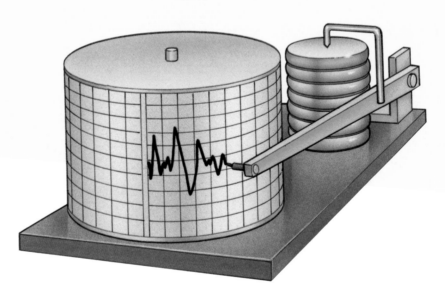

Seismometers record earthquake vibrations as movements of a needle on paper.

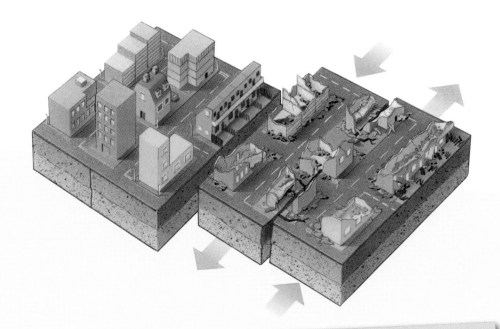

BEFORE AND AFTER

The diagram above shows a city before and after an earthquake. What has changed? What has stayed the same? What might be the reasons for the changes?

the tectonic plates slipped apart. Scientists measure from the spot where the slip started to the spot where it stopped. Scientists call this the rupture distance. Any earthquake that occurs within one or two rupture distances of the mainshock is classified as an aftershock.

How Earthquakes Happen

The shifting of Earth's seven major tectonic plates and dozens of smaller ones causes earthquakes. The movement of the Indian plate against the Eurasian plate caused the earthquake in Awaran. Movement of the Pacific and North American plates against each other causes earthquakes in California.

The plates are always undergoing extremely slow movement, forming new crust and grinding old rocks into particles of sand and dust. On the surface, the effects of this movement are most visible along fault lines.

The jagged edges of the plates make fault lines uneven. Uneven edges can get caught on each other. So even though the rest of the plate continues to move, the edges can sometimes stop. When they do, stress begins to build up below Earth's surface.

Finally, when the stress becomes too great, the plates grind against each other or one plate pushes above the

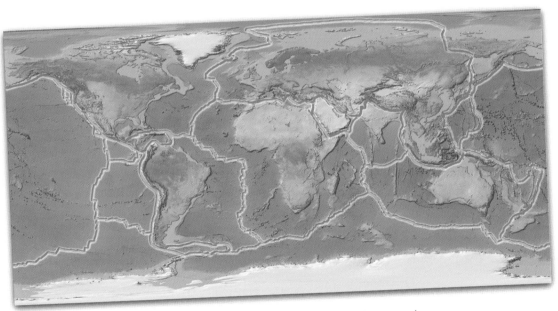

Scientists have discovered that Earth's crust is broken up into many shifting plates.

Seismic waves can rip the ground apart near an earthquake's epicenter.

other. The location where the stress is finally released is called the hypocenter. The hypocenter is where the earthquake starts. A **wave** of energy travels up to Earth's surface from the hypocenter. The spot on Earth's surface directly above the hypocenter is known as the epicenter.

The pressing, sliding, and grinding motion of the plates creates waves of energy called **seismic** waves. These waves ripple outward in all directions from the epicenter. They travel along the surface of Earth, causing the shaking of an earthquake.

PLATE TECTONICS

Plate tectonics is the theory that Earth's crust is made up of large, slowly moving plates. One of the earliest suggestions of the existence of plates came in 1596. A mapmaker named Abraham Ortelius noticed that the edges of the continents seemed to fit together. Centuries later, in 1912, German scientist Alfred Wegener had a similar idea. He believed Earth's continents had been joined as one supercontinent in the distant past. But other scientists rejected his idea, since Wegener had no explanation for how the continents had moved apart.

Scientists found evidence for the theory in the 1950s as people mapped the seafloor. They discovered ocean ridges, underwater mountains that form where continents had likely moved apart. Like many scientific theories, plate tectonics was not widely accepted at first. But after decades of study returned large amounts of evidence, scientists accepted the theory as the best explanation for the structure and movement of Earth's crust.

CHAPTER 4

EARTHQUAKE EFFECTS

Being in an earthquake can be terrifying. Without warning, the ground suddenly starts shaking under your feet. If you are outside, the quake could knock you to the ground. In a building, it may feel as though the structure will collapse. Things can fall from shelves or the ceiling. Even though earthquakes often last less than a minute, they can cause enormous damage.

During an earthquake, shaking causes damage in various ways. Different types of seismic waves have different effects. One kind is called a P wave. It shakes the ground from side to side. P waves are also called compressional waves because they compress and expand the earth as they travel. Another kind of seismic wave is called an S wave. It shakes the ground up and down. It causes an earthquake's rolling motion.

The amount of damage an earthquake causes has a lot to do with whether it happens in a populated area. If

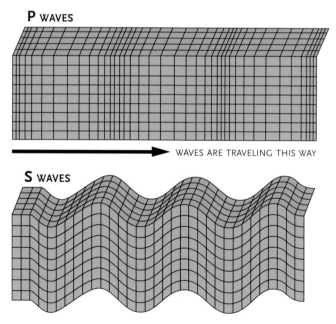

S waves travel more slowly than P waves, so people typically feel P waves first.

it happens far from a city, it may have little effect on people. But in populated areas, damage and danger can affect people greatly. Sometimes, the shaking damages structures directly. Other times, damage happens when the ground settles into a new position after the earthquake.

Powerful earthquakes can quickly reduce an entire area to rubble.

THE RING OF FIRE

Earthquake scientists know 90 percent of the world's earthquakes happen in a strip called the Ring of Fire. This strip winds around the Pacific Ocean, touching the coasts of North and South America, Japan, the Philippines, and the island nations north of Australia. Several different tectonic plates collide along the Ring of Fire. The area is also known for frequent volcanic eruptions.

Along coastlines, earthquakes can cause damage from flooding. Shaking can break dams or levees, letting water flow into streets and towns. Sometimes, the shaking of an earthquake that happens in the ocean floor can cause a **tsunami**. The shaking creates a wave in the water. A tsunami forms if the shaking of the earth beneath the ocean floor is up and down. This motion creates a tsunami wave. The tsunami wave grows larger as it moves, pulling water into itself. The giant wave rushes toward shore, flooding whatever is in its path.

Tsunami waves can devastate towns and cities on the coast.

Earthquakes can also cause a great deal of damage after the shaking is over. This was the case in the San Francisco earthquake of 1906. The earthquake caused underground water pipes to break. When a fire started after the earthquake, firefighters were unable to get water to put out the fire. Fires spread through the city. Engineers later designed water pipes that could survive an earthquake.

LIQUEFACTION

Liquefaction creates some of the most dangerous effects of earthquakes. It occurs when the shaking of the earth causes water in the ground to soak into surrounding soil. The soil begins to behave like a liquid, flowing instead of standing still and supporting structures above it. Without support, buildings, roads, and underground pipes can collapse.

Today, earthquake scientists work to prevent this kind of damage. They know that some areas have sandy soil, putting them at risk of liquefaction. Scientists use instruments to measure the soil. They drill deep into Earth to take samples. They want to see how sandy and dense the soil is. The scientists use their observations to tell engineers where it is safest to build.

CHAPTER 5

EARTHQUAKE SAFETY

Although they have learned much about earthquakes, scientists are not yet able to predict exactly when or where the next earthquake will be. As a result, the focus of earthquake safety is on earthquake **preparedness** rather than prediction. Earthquake scientists make recommendations to governments, engineers, and everyday people to help communities prepare for the effects of earthquakes.

One important safety step is a network of tsunami

warning systems along coastlines. Governments construct these systems to alert communities if an earthquake has triggered a tsunami nearby. This gives people time to move to high ground before the tsunami waves reach the shore.

Another important safety step is developing rules so that new roads and structures are strong enough to withstand an earthquake. Public buildings and bridges

Scientists set up equipment to measure earthquake effects, giving them a better idea of how earthquakes work.

Computer systems help scientists track tsunamis and save lives in affected areas.

that existed before the new rules went into effect can be upgraded so they will survive an earthquake, too. This process is known as retrofitting.

Many different factors affect how well structures survive earthquakes. Building shape is one factor. Square or rectangular buildings are often more stable during earthquakes than ones with rounded shapes. Materials are another factor. Flexible materials, such as steel and aluminum, are better at withstanding earthquakes than brittle materials, such as brick and stone. Flexible materials can move with the forces earthquakes create, rather than resisting the forces and breaking. Engineers must also pay attention to the kind of soil beneath buildings. If there is a risk of liquefaction, builders should construct a foundation designed to handle the shifting soil and prevent a collapse.

When comparing areas that have earthquake-ready building codes against areas without them, the difference in damage can be enormous. The 1994 Northridge earthquake in California had a magnitude of 6.7. It took

RETROFITTING

One way to minimize an earthquake's damage is to retrofit structures so that they are not destroyed during an earthquake. Structures built before the 1990s often must be strengthened so they can withstand an earthquake. Sturdy metal plates and beams are bolted onto the structure to anchor it to its foundation. That way, the structure will not slide off of its foundation during the shaking of an earthquake.

place in a densely populated area, but building regulations in the area were designed to protect against earthquakes. Sixty people died. Nine years later, a magnitude 6.6 earthquake hit Bam, Iran. The area did not have earthquake-ready building codes, and more than 30,000 people died. Careful engineering is the first step in preventing earthquake damage.

Families can also take steps to prepare for earthquakes. If water pipes and power lines are damaged, a family may be left without clean water and electricity. The Federal Emergency Management Agency recommends that families living in earthquake-prone areas always keep enough food, water, and other supplies on hand to last 72 hours after an earthquake.

Another major danger of earthquakes comes from falling objects that are knocked loose by shaking. To prevent injuries, families can fasten shelves securely to walls and hang heavy items, such as picture frames, away from couches or beds.

Preparation and planning could have saved lives in the Awaran earthquake and other similar disasters.

Knowing what to expect and what to do during an earthquake can keep you and your family safe. If you feel an earthquake, drop to the ground so that you do not fall down. Take cover under something sturdy, like a table or desk. If you cannot get under something strong, move to a corner and cover your head and face with your arms. If you are outside, move away from buildings and power lines.

Earthquakes are powerful forces of nature. As with the Awaran earthquake, they can be destructive, collapsing buildings, breaking apart roads, and killing or injuring many people. But their power is not only destructive. Earthquakes can also build mountains and create islands.

Earthquake scientists hope that by studying how and why earthquakes happen, they will become better at predicting where and when the next one will hit. Perhaps one day, scientists will be able to predict earthquakes. Until then, people must follow steps to reduce the danger from these deadly disasters.

THE SAN FRANCISCO EARTHQUAKE OF 1906

On April 18, 1906, near San Francisco, California, movement occurred at the **boundary** between plates, causing a huge earthquake. At that time, scientists did not know what caused earthquakes. But they were eager to learn more. Scientists all over California made observations. They took photographs, drew pictures, and wrote detailed notes. They climbed mountains to see how the earthquake had changed the surface of Earth. Scientists realized the worst damage was close to the fault line.

Today, scientists use observations to tell how much stress is building up along fault lines. They use satellite pictures to examine fault lines. They watch for changes. As the stress increases, they know that the risk of an earthquake is greater. They are able to use their observations to warn people that there may be an earthquake in the near future. Scientists are still unable to predict exactly when an earthquake will happen. But by studying earthquakes of the past, they become better and better at predicting earthquakes of the future.

TOP FIVE WORST
EARTHQUAKES

1. **Chile earthquake of 1960, Magnitude 9.5**
   This is the world's largest recorded earthquake. About 1,650 people died. The earthquake created a tsunami and caused damage in Hawaii, Japan, the Philippines, and the West Coast of the United States.

2. **Alaska earthquake of 1964, Magnitude 9.2**
   This earthquake began in Prince William Sound. It lasted more than four minutes and was felt in Oregon and California. Altogether, 131 people died.

3. **Northern Sumatra earthquake of 2004, Magnitude 9.1**
   Almost 228,000 people died in this earthquake and the tsunami that it created. The worst destruction was seen in South Asia and East Africa.

4. **Japan earthquake and tsunami of 2011, Magnitude 9.0**
   This earthquake and the resulting tsunami killed more than 15,000 people. Severe damage occurred at the nuclear power plant in Fukushima, Japan, causing radioactive leaks into the Pacific Ocean.

5. **Kamchatka, Russia earthquake of 1952, Magnitude 9.0**
   Most of the destruction caused by this Russian earthquake was from the tsunami it created. The tsunami flooded parts of Alaska and even caused flooding as far away as Hawaii. Because the earthquake occurred in an area of low population, no lives were lost.

LEARN MORE

FURTHER READING

Griffey, Harriet. *Earthquakes and Other Natural Disasters*. New York: DK Children, 2010.

Mooney, Carla. *Earthquakes*. Minneapolis, MN: Abdo Publishing, 2013.

Simon, Seymour. *Earthquakes*. New York: HarperCollins, 2006.

Than, Ker. *Earthquakes*. New York: Scholastic, 2009.

WEB SITES

Discovery Kids—What Causes Earthquakes?
http://kids.discovery.com/tell-me/curiosity-corner/earth/natural-disasters/how-earthquakes-work
This Web site explains what happens during an earthquake.

US Geological Survey—Earthquakes for Kids
http://earthquake.usgs.gov/learn/kids
This Web site has activities, project ideas, and information about earthquakes.

GLOSSARY

boundary (BOUN-duh-ree) a dividing line

fault lines (FAWLT linez) breaks in Earth's crust

magnitude (MAG-nuh-tood) the intensity of an earthquake represented by a number on a scale

preparedness (pre-PAIR-ed-ness) the quality or state of being prepared

rupture (RUHP-chur) a breaking or tearing

seismic (SIZE-mic) related to an earthquake or another shaking of Earth

tsunami (tsoo-NAH-mee) a large wave caused by the shaking of an earthquake

wave (WAYV) the movement of energy through a material

INDEX